THE
MIRACLE

Little Girl Lost in the Woods

DON R. BROWN

ISBN 978-1-957943-42-8 (paperback)
ISBN 978-1-957943-43-5 (hardcover)
ISBN 978-1-957943-44-2 (digital)

Rushmore Press LLC
1 800 460 9188
www.rushmorepress.com

Printed in the United States of America

I have seen a lot of things in my life that are not scientifically possible. The first thing that happened was when I was 7 years old. I was on the school bus, close to my stop. A girl was ahead of me. Her mother had been waiting in the car. When I got off, there was an older boy waiting to talk to me. There was no one before the bus stopped. He wanted to talk to me as I headed up the street. I lived about 3 blocks up the street. As we walked, he asked me how my brothers and sisters were doing. Then he asked about my parents. I asked him how he knew my parents. He said, "I know everyone in your family." I had no answer for that. As we walked, we came to the first side street. There was only one house on that street. It was about 1/2 blocks away. He said, "I'm going down this way." He didn't say he lived there. I continued to walk about 5 steps up the street and turned and looked to see how far he had gotten. He was nowhere in sight. That was impossible. I thought that I would talk to him the next day. I never saw him again. He must have been an angel.

I love to see things happen that are not what we would expect. When I was 5 years old, I was sure that time was an illusion of some type. I was sure of it at the time. When I was 7, I had been to a few western movies. I wanted a holster for my cap pistol. We had a pair of leather boots that my father was not going to use anymore. I cut one of the boots so that I had a good size piece of leather for a cap pistol. I drew around the gun with a marker that I had and made it large enough for hanging on it a belt. I used a leather punch that my father had to make the holes in the edge to tie with a leather shoestring. Just after I was done, a friend of mine came over to see me. He asked where I bought the holster. I told him that I made it. He didn't believe me. I had to show him how I made it. I felt good knowing he was impressed. Later, I wondered how I was able to make something like that without even thinking about it. Maybe it was from a past life. I first started wondering about this life at about 6 years old. At that time, I wondered how far out you could go if you were able to fly at the speed of light into outer space. I thought that there couldn't be an end to it. On the other hand, how could it go on forever? I knew then that we don't know a lot of things about this life.

I lived in Bend, Ore. I had driven to the Salem area to help a driver unload some furniture. On the way back, I was going up the mountain highway and I heard a voice in my head saying, "Slow down." I thought, why should I slow down? I drove another 100 feet and the voice said, "If you don't slow down, you will have to tell your wife that you wrecked the car." I thought, "Ok, I will slow down to 20 mph. I came around the curve just ahead of me and a deer walked out in front of me. I would have done something bad if I hadn't slowed down. I sure didn't want to run into a deer. I think everyone can receive messages like that, but some people would not pay attention. A lady who I worked with once told me that she was driving on a 2-lane highway and turned to say something to her child in the back seat. She looked back at the highway and was on the wrong side of the road. There was a car coming toward her. She closed her eyes because she knew she would die in a second. She opened her eyes after a few seconds because nothing happened. She was on the right side of the road. I heard a similar story from two other people. I think people die only when it is their time. I had an experience with dying once also. I was about 49. My wife and I had been at a lake with our boat. The song "American Pie" told the story of that experience very well. We went to a lake that we had been to many times before. The water was about 5 feet lower than it usually was. We got to the other side of the lake on our boat and there were 2 men sitting on the shore drinking whiskey from pint bottles. We got there in my "chevy pickup." When we got home, I told my wife that I didn't feel well. She said I should take a bath. I got in the tub and felt strange. I got into bed and felt even worse. I got up and went to the living room and told my wife and her son that I didn't feel good. "I need to go to a doctor." I turned to go to get dressed and woke up on the floor. The paramedics came and I was still laying down. They got me to the sitting up position and I left my body. I went down a "tunnel" like others say when they have a "near-death experience." When I got to the end of the tunnel, I stepped down. I was wearing a long white robe. The first thing I thought was, "We've lived here for 5 years and I didn't know this room was here." There was a door on the left. A man (dressed the same as I) was standing at the door. There were people coming through the door. The man was saying, "For those of you who just arrived—" I looked ahead. There was a man who looked like Jesus who was standing at the end of a long wooden picnic table. There were about 10 people sitting on either side. He was saying, "When you go out among the people—" That was all that I could remember when I came back to my body. The next thing I remember was how I felt. I felt that I was back home. I was like a little kid. I never wanted to leave. I have never felt that good in this life. I think that is why babies are so happy. They came from a very nice place. The next thing I knew was I heard a paramedic calling my name from 50 feet away. Then I heard him call my name from right next to me. I was wishing that I could have stayed where I was at. I was taken to a hospital. The doctor told my wife that I probably wouldn't make it through the night. My wife told me that the next day. A couple of people from our church came and gave me a blessing the next day. The doctor took a quart of water from the sack around my heart the night before. The next day, he put a fiber-optic tube into each of my lungs. He started stuttering. He couldn't believe that there was nothing wrong with my lungs. I found that I had been walking around for a week with pneumonia and didn't know it. I got better in a few days and was able to go back to work. That was 30 years ago. I was always thankful for that experience of leaving my body. I am not afraid of dying now. I never was concerned with it much, but I am sure now.

Dreams—When I was on the road in my truck, I had a dream one night at home. In the dream, I was going down a highway and turned to the right to go over a bridge across a river. On the other side of the bridge, there was a pickup parked on the side of the road. The road turned to the left and went uphill from there. Because of the way the road turned to the right about 1/8th of a mile up the hill, I was able to imagine that you could run off the edge of the road if you used your imagination. About 8 days later, I was on a highway that I had never been on before heading for northern California. I was shocked to recognize the bridge ahead of me. It was the one that I had seen in my dream. As I got to the end of the bridge, there was the pickup. I went around the curve to the left and the highway went up the hill with the curve to the right. Just like my dream. I had another dream where I met another truck coming toward me. I saw the same truck about a week later when I went on my next trip. I had a very interesting dream each month for about 10 years. In this dream, I was walking across a highway bridge and the concrete kept falling from the roadway. I finally had to walk on the side of the bridge on a metal beam. In my dream, I never got to the other side of the waterway.

After 10 years of having this dream, I was heading down I-5 in my truck and listening to a public broadcasting station on the radio. A lady was telling a story about her grandfather. He lived in Japan when it was bombed by the U.S. She described my dream exactly. She said he was walking across the bridge and had to walk on a steel beam because the rest of the pavement had crumbled into the water. He was determined to get to the other side because he wanted to make sure his daughters were OK. They were fine. I always wished that I had stopped to call the radio station. I didn't have a cell phone at the time. It was before they were invented. When I called the radio station years later, they didn't know who the lady was.

We lived out of town between the Oregon Caves and Grants Pass. We moved a lot as I was growing up. My father couldn't stand living in one place for more than a couple of years. I did not like moving and my brothers and sisters probably did not like it either. One thing that bothered me was that I would just get to know some friends at school and we would have to move and start all over again. We usually lived out of town also. That way, there was no chance of getting a job during the summer. We started in Eugene. From there, we moved to Loraine, then to Pistol River, Gold Beach, and Brookings. That is where my youngest sister Dorothy was born. She was only a little over a year old when we moved to the Wonder, Or. area. It was late in November, 1956. The weather had been getting cold at night (5degrees). There was already some snow on the ground where the sun failed to penetrate during the day. I could feel the chill in the air as my brother Delbert and I chopped wood for the fireplace. "Looks like winter is here for sure," he said as he swung the ax again.

I was the next to the oldest of seven children, ranging from 1&1/2 to 16 years old. We lived about a mile from the highway. There were old logging units with second-growth timber and many old logging roads surrounding the house. The nearest town was Grants Pass, about 8 miles away. The area where we lived was called Wonder. There was a gas station and a store and that was about it.

Mom called from the house to ask if we knew where Dorothy was. She was our youngest sister (1&1/2 years old). "No," I answered back. We were about to continue our wood-cutting chore when Mom called again—"I looked all through the house for her and I can't find her anywhere. You boys had better look around for her outside." My brother started around the house to look in the back. I decided to look in the cooler room in the house. There was no cooler unit, but there was a thick cooler door in the room. I had gotten locked in the room at one time accidentally.

Fortunately, my sister was there to hear me yell and let me out. It was not cold, but there was a possibility that you could be there for a long time before anyone would think to check inside. We stored some things inside. "She isn't here, I yelled." I knew she had to be somewhere close by. After all, how far could a child who had only been walking for a short time have gotten in a few minutes? I would certainly live to regret my underestimation of my sister. I still do not know how she did what she did.

At Mom's suggestion, Delbert and I made a circle around the house at about a hundred-yard radius. We looked down all the logging roads and into all of the clearings, but to no avail. I even walked along the main road past our house (a dirt road, like the rest of them) for a way but saw no sign of her.

As we started back toward the house to check with Mom, Dad returned from town with one of my sisters. I think we were all a little relieved to see him. He always knew what to do—or so it seemed to a 14-year-old. His eyes showed concern as Mom related the events of the past few minutes. "How long has she been gone?" he asked.

"About ten minutes," she said. I could tell that they were both worried now. "Go down to the neighbors and call the State Police," Dad told me. "The rest of us will start looking now." I promptly walked to the neighbor's house (he was also our landlord). He brought me back in his pickup.

The Police wasted no time in getting there. After speaking briefly with Dad, they organized a search. The first place they looked was a well, not far from the house. This was something I couldn't watch. Many horrible pictures ran through my mind in the short time it took them to finish. There was nothing in the well. That was very good news.

Word had gotten out to the neighbors by this time that a little girl had gotten lost in the woods. I don't know how they knew. I think a local TV or radio station had gotten word about the situation. There were people everywhere. Some of them carried flashlights because it would be dark soon. The police brought out some bloodhounds. I thought that the dogs would find her soon. Mom bought out a dress that she had worn recently. The dogs seemed to be confused. They would go for a short way, then backtrack on their own trail. I think this was because of the large number of people in the area.

It was getting dark now. It had been an hour since Mom had last seen little Dorothy. The coming of darkness only increased my fears as I kept looking. I kept silently praying as I searched among the trees. I kept hoping to hear a shout of "We found her," but it didn't come. For the first time in my life, I was grateful that my parents had taught me to believe in God. I knew that he wouldn't let anything happen to such a young and innocent child as Dorothy. I hoped that the presence of so many people would keep the wild animals scared off. My father and I had seen some cougar tracks a week or so before. I knew that a cougar wouldn't get too close to people if they could help it.

Though the evening's events were a terrible shock to me, I was still able to be of assistance in the search. Mom was taking it pretty hard, though she tried not to show it for the benefit of us children. A minister tried to comfort her, but what could anyone say at a time like this? Mom and Dad both had tears in their eyes around 10 o'clock when we still hadn't found a trace of Dorothy. We all tried to keep our hopes up, but as time went by, there seemed to be less and less chance of finding her alive. The temperature had been dropping steadily since the sun went down. Before morning, it would reach 5 degrees F. When it gets this cold in Oregon, the wind seems to go right through you. I shivered under the heavy jacket that I wore. "How," I thought, "could a child with only a nightgown on survive in this weather?"

Again, I thought about the things I had heard in Sunday school. By this time, I knew that God was our only hope.

"God is merciful," they said. "He loves all little children." Surely, he would watch over her. Only he knew where she was. My thoughts went back to a time when I was 9 years old. I had been hunting with my dad. He suggested that we go on slightly different routes as we headed for home. He always knew what direction he was going. I didn't. I had other abilities, but not that one. I soon became helplessly lost. I shouted for my father but got no answer. I remembered hearing that a person should remain calm if they were lost. My brother Delbert was with me. He did not know where to go either. I stopped and knelt down and prayed to God to show us the way. I stood up and for some reason, pointed a certain direction and said to Delbert "this way." We walked about 40 feet or so when I saw a road that I recognized. I have never forgotten that incident. I believe that if you believe in what you are asking, it will work out for you. I was not sure at the time if it was a coincidence or if my prayer was answered. I think it was the latter.

It was around midnight now. Light snow was falling. Occasionally, we took a break to reorganize and to grab a hot cup of coffee. It helped to ward off the cold, but it also made me wonder how long Dorothy would be able to survive out there before her body stopped functioning.

Everyone had run out of ideas as to where to look. Dad and I had been to the main highway. It was a mile away. My worst fear was that when we found her, she would be in a place that I had passed by closely and not seen her for some reason.

My younger brother and sisters were too young to realize the tragedy of the situation, but they stayed up waiting for us to find their sister. I didn't say too much to Delbert. I knew he felt the same way as I did. Though we weren't what you would call a close-knit family, we were always concerned for each other.

Dad and I had once again reached the road that led to the highway. "Going on one o'clock," he said without feeling. "Wait, I thought I heard something!" Then we heard it loud and clear. "We found her." Then in a moment, "She is alive!" Dad and I hurried in the direction from which the shouting had come. They were putting her into a car to rush her to the hospital. We were so happy we didn't know what to do. We wanted to know who had found her so that we could shake their hand.

It was the minister who had found her. She was on a logging road a quarter of a mile from the house, in the opposite direction from the highway. She was still toddling along. "She didn't even cry until I picked her up," the minister said. When he found her, he immediately opened his shirt and put her feet against his stomach to warm them, possibly saving her from frostbite. He said he had been praying all night and knew that God would help him find her. She was a quarter of a mile farther in that direction than we had looked. We knew that she couldn't have possibly walked that far. Sometimes, logic does not work. I do not know how she did it. Keeping moving saved her, that is for sure.

She was kept in the hospital until the next day. Despite her nine-hour ordeal, and a mild case of shock, she was fine. We will always be grateful for all the people who helped in the search. Thanks to them, Dorothy survived being lost in the woods. She lived in her early 50s when she died from smoking too much. It was truly a miracle that she was able to keep walking for 5 or 6 hours. I assumed that is what happened. The outcome was good anyway. I am not sure what happens when the outcome is something that you wouldn't believe in a movie. I have since talked to other people who have had things happen that are unexplainable. I am sure glad that this was one of those times. I think that a person will not die if it is not their time to go. There is a lot to this life that we don't know. I like knowing that.